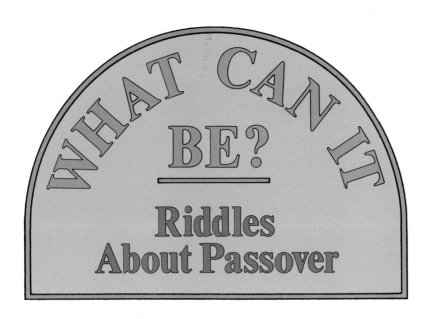

WHAT CAN IT BE?

Riddles About Passover

By Susan Cornell Poskanzer

Original Photography by Rob Gray

Silver Press

Published by Silver Press, a division of
Silver Burdett Press, Inc.
Simon & Schuster, Inc.
Prentice Hall Bldg., Englewood Cliffs, NJ 07632.

Printed in the United States of America.

Library of Congress Cataloging-in-Publication Data

Poskanzer, Susan Cornell.
Riddles about Passover / by Susan C. Poskanzer.
p.   cm.   (What can it be?)
Summary: A collection of non-humorous riddles relating to the
historical background of Passover and the way this day is celebrated.
1. Passover——Juvenile literature.   2. Riddles, Juvenile.
[1. Passover.   2. Riddles.]   I. Title.   II. Series.
BM695.P3P67   1991   296.4′ 37——dc20
ISBN 0-671-72725-7   90-39412
ISBN 0-671-72724-9 (lib. bdg.)   CIP
                                                       AC

WHAT CAN IT BE? concept created by Jacqueline A. Ball.
Thomas Goddard/Goddard Design, Design Consultant
Thanks to: Susan and Sam Chwat and Cantor Irwin Gelman
Photographs of Red Sea and Sinai Desert © Superstock, Inc.;
photograph of pyramids (Egypt) courtesy of Beth Waitkus

Long ago in Egypt,
where pyramids still stand,
a king was called a pharaoh,
and he ruled a mighty land.
The Jews were slaves for ages.
They worked without a break,
until a man named Moses said
it was a big mistake.
He called on Pharaoh Ramses.
He said, "Let my people go!"
I celebrate their freedom,
for at last they won, you know.

What holiday am I?

PASSOVER

Passover is a Jewish holiday that celebrates freedom
and new life. When the Egyptian king wouldn't free
the Jews, God had the Jews mark their doors with blood
from a roasted lamb before sending ten plagues as
punishment. Then God "passed over" the marked houses
without harming the people in them. Later Moses led
the Jews across the desert to freedom.

Search any globe to find me,
I'm sure that you'll agree:
I lie just east of Egypt.
I'm a long and windy sea.
In history, I'm famous.
I'm sure you know it's true.
And even though my name is red,
my water looks quite blue.

What am I?

THE RED SEA OR THE SEA OF REEDS

As the Jews left Egypt, Pharaoh's army chased them. When the Red Sea blocked the Jews, they felt all was lost. But a miracle happened when God parted the waters and the Jewish people walked across the dry land to freedom.

A great and mighty nation,
a proud and handsome land,
my story's filled with pharaohs.
My deserts? Filled with sand!
I have the ancient pyramids.
I have the great Red Sea.
So if you want to see them,
just come and visit me.

What am I?

EGYPT

In ancient times, Egypt was a very powerful,
rich country. Many Jews had moved to Egypt
when it was hard to find food elsewhere.
They lived there peacefully until Pharaoh took
away their freedom and made them slaves.

I was a king, quite long ago,
in Egypt, my home state,
when Moses came
to talk with me,
and said he couldn't wait.
He told me I should free the slaves.
How could I ever know. . .
that things would
get so awful
when I didn't let them go?

Who am I?

PHARAOH RAMSES

The Jewish leader Moses asked the Egyptian Pharaoh Ramses to free the Jews. While he was king, Ramses had a new Egyptian capital and many great temples built.

We came to the land
where the pharaoh was grand.
We hopped on six legs,
and we flew.
We spoiled the crops,
and we just wouldn't stop
'til we'd eaten them all
through and through.

What were we?

LOCUSTS

The ten plagues God sent down on the Egyptians were locusts that ate the crops growing in the fields, water that turned to blood, frogs, lice, wild beasts, cattle disease, boils, hail, darkness, and death.

Chicken soup,
cups of wine,
matzah balls,
all so fine.
Songs to sing.
Time to pray.
Aunts to hug.
Lots to say.
I'm a feast.
Come and eat.
Join the fun.
Have a treat.

What am I?

A SEDER OR PASSOVER FEAST

Seders are held on the first two nights of Passover.
Seder means "order" and everything is done
in a special order at a seder. During a seder the
story of the Jews' freedom is told, prayers
are said, songs are sung, and good food is eaten.
It is a custom to invite to the seder anyone
who may feel alone on the holiday.

We start the seder.
We're warm and we're bright.
We shimmer and shine
on the table at night.
We stand very proud.
We're a wonderful sight.
We throw dancing shadows
with glistening light.

What are we?

CANDLES

Lighting the candles is the first thing to do at a seder. Usually the mother says a prayer as she lights two or more candles. The candles stay lit for the entire dinner and service.

I'm a holiday book,
as perhaps you will see.
At the Passover feast,
everybody reads me.
Listen, and hear
all that I have to tell,
and you'll learn the story
of Passover well.

What am I?

A HAGGADAH

The haggadah is the book used at the Passover seder. Haggadah means "telling" in Hebrew. The book has stories, songs, prayers, and directions for the Passover service.

I'm flat, and I'm golden.
I crunch when you chew.
I'm Passover bread
that is tasty; it's true.
You may want to bake me.
I'm part of the feast.
Add flour and water,
but leave out the yeast.

What am I?

MATZAH

When Pharaoh freed the Jews, they left quickly. Since there was no time to let their raw dough rise, they simply took it with them. Later the dough baked into flat sheets in the hot desert sun. Today Jews eat only matzah, or flat bread without yeast, during the days of Passover.

I'm set out on the table
for quite a special meal.
I hold five ancient symbols
that just may be ideal.
For at the family seder,
so many look to me.
I help them to remember
it's splendid to be free!

What am I?

THE SEDER PLATE

The seder plate holds five things: A roasted lamb bone stands for the lamb roasted on the night of the first Passover. A roasted egg and greens, like parsley, stand for spring when new life begins. Bitter herbs, like horseradish, stand for bitter slavery. Haroset, a mix of apples, nuts, cinnamon, and wine, looks like mortar the slaves used to hold bricks together.

You'll find me in the ocean.
It's easy as can be.
I'm what your tears are made of.
Just taste me and you'll see.

What am I?

SALT WATER

During the seder, people usually taste salt water. This reminds them of the tears cried by slaves in Egypt.

עֲבָדִים הָיִינוּ לְפַרְעֹה בְּמִצְרָיִם

מַיִם מָלוּחַ

I come after winter,
year after year,
when new lambs, and robins,
and young chicks appear.
A time to start planting,
or building a nest,
I'm such a fine season,
you may like me best.

What am I?

SPRING

Passover comes
in the spring
and celebrates
freedom and the
beginning of new
life.

I'm one of many at the feast,
the smallest you may see.
But I ask four big questions.
I'm important as can be.
I ask about the reasons
that we celebrate these days,
and why they are quite special
in so very many ways.

Who am I?

THE YOUNGEST CHILD AT THE SEDER

At the seder the youngest child who is able asks the Four Questions. The Four Questions ask the reasons for the Passover holiday. The seder leader answers by telling the story of how God helped the Jews out of slavery in Egypt and led them to Israel.

I'm one half of a matzah,
a game of hide and seek.
The leader gets to hide me.
The children never peek.
Then later when they find me,
the kids are always wise.
They always keep me with them
until they get a prize.

What am I?

THE AFIKOMAN

The Afikoman is half of a matzah that the leader hides. Later, when it is needed, the children search for it. When they find the Afikoman, they give it back . . . only after they've bargained for a prize. Afikoman is a Greek word that means "dessert." It is the last food eaten at the seder.

A beautiful cup,
I'm always filled up
for a wonderful part of the seder.
Holding holiday wine,
I look ever so fine,
and I welcome a guest who comes later.

What am I?

ELIJAH'S CUP

During the seder an extra cup is filled with wine for the prophet Elijah. A prophet is a very wise man of God. Elijah symbolizes hope and peace for the whole world. Near the end of the seder, a door is opened so that Elijah and peace may come in.